The Purpose Factor

A Guided Journal to

Living a Life of Purpose

Jacqueline Evans-Phillips

Copyright © 2014 Dr. Jacqueline Evans-Phillips
All rights reserved. This book, or parts thereof, must not be reproduced without written permission of this writer and/or her designee.
Printed in the United States
ISBN: 10: 1533335214
ISBN-13: 978-1533335210
First published 2016

DEDICATION

To Teresa James, you are the wind beneath my wings;
my mom, Marcella Evans, my prayer warrior;
and my children,
Xavier & Angelique;
you mean the world to me

TABLE OF CONTENTS

Acknowledgments	6
Introduction	7
Pre-Assessment	11
SECTION ONE	13
What is Purpose?	14
SECTION TWO	17
First Principle:	
Activating Your Push Power **(APP)**	19
Second Principle:	
Developing the Whole Self **(DWS)**	49
What is Your Mission Statement?	51
Third Principle:	
Enhancing Love in all Relationships **(ELR)**	83
Fourth Principle:	
Being of Service **(BS)**	121
SECTION THREE	151
Your Combined Engagement Score	151
The Trauma Factor **(TF)**	157
Your Three to Six Month Road Map Journey	
Begins Here: Worksheets	163
Developing Your Road Map	166
Developing SMART Goals	176
Your Next Steps	184
Reflections	185
Glossary of Terms	212
About the Author	214

ACKNOWLEDGMENTS

My Village, my support, my friends: thanks for pushing and encouraging me. It takes a Village to make a difference.

Special thanks to Vangella H. Buchanan for editing and layout
Joyce LeBaron for editing services
Tracy Lyn Designs LLC. for book cover design

Introduction

Pressure, as illustrated by the Webster's Dictionary, is the application of force to something by something else in direct contact with it. This application of force can be compared to the pressure we feel in our lives as we go through trials and tribulations. Sometimes in life, we may feel that we are taking one step forward and two steps backward. Many times, we turn to God and ask the question, "Why?" "Will this pressure ever disappear?" "Why me, Lord?" are phrases we may utter when the pain comes crashing down on us.

Two years ago, I became the victim of an employment layoff. I received a year's notice, since my position was being eliminated due to a reorganization. By God's grace, it has been five months since the effect of that notice and, thus far, I am still employed under temporary contracts. This rapid change drastically shifted my whole world. I felt as if I was in the spin cycle of a washing machine with the ever-present threat of someone opening the washing machine door while the wash was in progress. This storm has been one in which I became uncertain of my financial security and the manner in which I was going to provide for my family.

Through this storm, I was fully pressed into **Purpose**. The pressure of this adversity fully submerged me into my **Call to Greatness**. I am the author of this book, **The Purpose Factor** and a co-author in another called **Stand Up to be Heard Vol. 2.** Also during this season, I have started my own company Life Changers Consulting. Through my company, I am able to coach and empower individuals towards living a **Life of Purpose**. This adversity has strengthened my faith and I stand in awe of God's greatness and the manner in which he uses adversity to position us into **Greatness**. He has designed us to be his vessel for his greater glory to fulfil our purpose on this earth.

The manner in which we are able to quickly manage our daily pressures will determine our recovery period and our mental equilibrium. My journey of walking into my **Purpose** or my **Call to Greatness** was not an easy one. I am a work in progress while I am still pressing towards the mark of a **Purposeful Life**. Along this journey, I have developed several principles that have taught me how to navigate through as well as manage my trials.

In this book, I will share principles that have guided me towards my journey of **Living a Purposeful Life**. Through this guided journal **The Purpose Factor,** you will develop a **Road Map** towards living a **Life of Purpose**. Over the past twenty-five years, journaling has been a tool I have used in designing a **Purposeful Life**. This is an intentional action towards taking my life to the next level; taking steps in walking toward my **Call to Greatness** by making a difference in the lives of others. Through this guided journal process, you will understand your **Call to Greatness** by:

1. Exploring the four principles to **Living a Life of Purpose** by:

   ❖ Strengthening your wings to **Connect with your Spirit**, your inner voice, or for some, the vibrations of the universe. As a Christian, it is my connection with the Holy Spirit, the force of God that is the energy which comes into my life and changes me.

   ❖ Understanding **Who You Are**, regarding your career, talents, gifts, and abilities, and then mapping out goals to enhance these talents and achieve success and balance in your life.

- ❖ **Enhancing your Relationships** with others by demonstrating love in all your personal interactions.

- ❖ **Being of Service** by spreading love and acts of kindness within your community. Through this process, you are able to make a difference in the lives of others.

2. Discover your current **Purpose Engagement** score, which will give you an insight into the areas of your life you can strengthen to move into a **Purpose Filled Life**. Through this journey, you will be able to design a **Road Map**, reflect, reassess, and affirm your goals and vision for this journey and the rest of your life. This process will consist of weekly activities to strengthen your **Road Map** goals.

3. Develop a strategic plan for the next three to six months beyond this book that will strengthen your **Purpose Filled** goals.

Finally, I welcome you to the **Purpose Factor Movement**. Join our movement of individuals who are intentionally working towards making a difference in their lives. Please connect and share your journey with us by signing up through our website: **www.thepurposefactormovement.com**.

Blessings,

Dr. Jacqueline Evans-Phillips

Special Note to Educators

This book can be used in an individual, group, or classroom setting. *The Purpose Factor* is a book that inspires and motivates individuals of all ages to begin **Living a Life of Purpose**.

The activities and themes can be modified to address specific age and types of group settings. Please visit my website at:

www.thepurposefactormovement.com for more information.

Pre-Assessment

Before we begin, let's do a quick self-assessment.

- **Are you living a Life of Purpose? Yes or No** *(circle one)*
- **How can you take your life to the next level?**

_____
_____
_____
_____
_____
_____
_____
_____
_____
_____
_____
_____
_____
_____
_____
_____
_____

- What are the factors that keep you from making this happen?

___

We would like to share this journey with you.
Please connect with us at:
www.thepurposefactormovement.com

SECTION ONE

WHAT IS PURPOSE?

Purpose is the reason something or someone was created or why it exists.

To **Live a Life of Purpose**, your actions have to be intentional. Ask yourself:
- Am I ready to live more authentically?
- Am I ready to master self-doubt and develop a mission statement to live by?
- Am I walking in my **Call to Greatness**?

In this book, I will take you on a journey of living a **Purpose-filled** life where you will begin to explore walking in your **Call to Greatness**. Your **Call to Greatness** is a vision for life where you truly understand the reason you were created. This understanding will give you a new lens through which to see your life, your relationships, and the world around you. My **Call to Greatness** is to make a difference in the lives of others. This **Greatness** is further chronicled with the development of my company **Life Changers Consulting** and the writing of this book. Through this process, I have developed the **Call to Greatness Empowerment Model**, which will help you make the transition into **Living a Life of Purpose**.

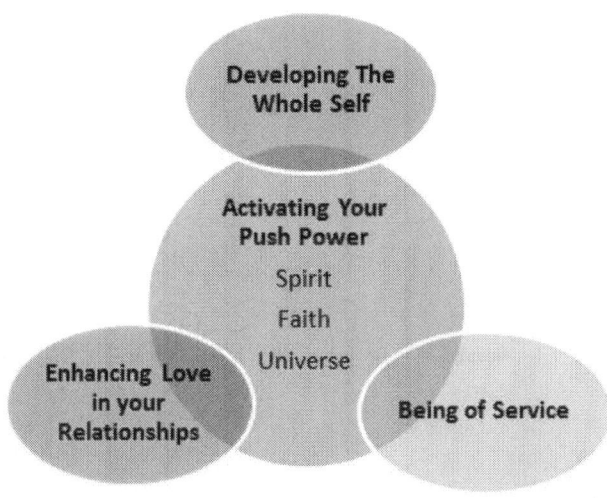

Figure 1.0 *Call to Greatness Empowerment Model*

As figure 1.0 illustrates, there are four principles to the **Call to Greatness Empowerment Model**: **Activating Your Push Power (APP), Developing the Whole Self (DWS), Enhancing Love in all Your Relationships (ELR)** and **Being of Service (BS)**.

To truly experience a **Life of Purpose**, the interplay of all four principles is critical. Your **APP** plays a dominant role in this model, whereby it activates the other three principles, **DWS, ELR** and **BS** into gear. Your **APP** is driven by the amount of energy and purpose you put into each principle. To assist you in activating a **Life of Purpose**, I have designed a performance scale where you can measure your level of engagement in each of the principles described below. You can engage from a level of 0 to 5 within each principle.

- Operating at a **level five** means that you are mastering that principle; you are intentional and engaged in actions that promote your strengths, talents and passion, love, and service to others. In addition, you are taking actions that promote continuous advancement, assessments, and reflections within that principle.

- Operating at a **level three** means that you are aware of your strengths, passion, or career interest. You are not consistently demonstrating love in all your relationships and may engage occasionally in some type of service to others. On that level, you have a conscious awareness of what to do to increase your performance and you may be taking strides toward success in that area.

- Operating at a **level zero** or **one** means that there isn't any type of activity or very little within that principle. This phase is called the **Trauma Factor (T- Factor),** where you may be experiencing some type of hardship in your life such as unemployment, homelessness, etc., or you are unclear of your direction regarding career, passion, or strengths. Please visit the Resources page on our website at **www.thepurposefactormovement.com** to take a self-discovery assessment.

The **T-Factor** will be described in greater detail, later in the book. In the meantime, if you are facing some type of trauma (hardship), I would like you to connect with your local Social Services for additional support. In order to move to a state of **Purpose,** you have to ensure that your basic needs are first met. According to *Maslow's Hierarchy of Needs*, one may be able to reach one's highest level of self-motivation, called **Self-Actualization**, when one's basic needs are met.

In this book, you will have the opportunity to discover your engagement level using the **Call to Greatness Empowerment Model**. By intentionally engaging in three or more of the **Call to Greatness Empowerment** principles, you will activate your success **Road Map**.

SECTION TWO

First Principle

Activating Your Push Power (APP)

First Principle: Activating Your Push Power (APP)

Your **Push Power** is your core to living a **Life of Purpose**. It is the drive and activating force for purpose. Without the **Push Power**, there will be no purpose. Your **Push Power** will give you the drive to pursue and develop a **Road Map** to accomplish your dreams.

The source of this **Push Power** is your Spirit, faith, or connection to the universe. As a Christian, it is my connection with the Holy Spirit, the force of God, the energy which comes into my life and changes me. The connection to the spirit is central to your success formula. The spirit in our life acts as a thermostat. Engaging the spirit will regulate the highs and lows in our lives as we ride through the waves of life.

The final manifestation of **Purpose** and the activation of your **Road Map** for success will be the demonstration of the **Fruit of the Spirit** within your life which is as follows: **Love, Joy, Peace, Patience, Kindness, Goodness, Faithfulness, Gentleness, Self-control** (Galatians 5:22-23). This **Fruit of the Spirit** I also classify as attributes **to Living a Life of Purpose**. These attributes will flow throughout all the principles of the **Call to Greatness Empowerment Model** and create a sense of harmony and balance within you, as well as within the people you share your gifts and talents with.

Strengthening your Push Power

Your connection to the spirit and activating the **Gifts of the Spirit** within you is critical to your purpose. In order to strengthen your engagement level in your **Push Power,** you will need to do the following:

1. Listen to the Spirit or the inner voice within you or, for some, the vibrations of the universe. This listening process will ignite a spark to enable you to push forward. For some,

this process may come more quickly than for others. Therefore, getting into the habit of a quiet, meditative state will enable you to reflect and discover your vision for your **Purpose**.

2. After you've listened to this voice, you will need to be obedient and follow the directions given. Write down the plan and you will see how the universe aligns with that voice in helping you achieve your goals. Through this vital spark, your connection process will activate the gifts and talents within you to make a difference in this world. (If you are unsure of your strengths, please visit the Resources page on our website at **www.thepurposefactormovement.com** to complete an assessment.)

Reflections

How would you describe your **Push Power** (drive) in pursuing your personal goals? Rate your engagement level of performance within this principle, using the following scale: 0 to 5

- Operating at a **level five** means that you are mastering that principle; you are intentional and engaged in actions that connect you to the spirit. You are engaging in meditational activities etc. In addition, you are writing and developing a **Road Map**, taking actions that promote continuous advancement, assessments, and reflections within that principle.
- Operating at a **level three** means that you are aware of your connection to the spirit and developing a **Road Map** for success. At this level, you are not consistently connecting daily to the spirit although you have a conscious awareness of what to do to increase your performance.
- Operating at a **level zero** or **one** means that there isn't any type of activity or very little within that principle.

Rate your performance in this Push Power principle, below using the following rubric:

Poor	Fair	Good	Very Good	Excellent
0	1	2	4	5

Your Push Power level of performance is _____

- o **Are you satisfied with your performance? Yes** *or* **No** (circle one)
- o **What are the factors that are either contributing to or impacting your Push Power (drive) performance?**

Developing your Road Map Plans

1. How can you master this principle over the next week?
2. What are one or two activities that you can engage in within the coming week that will increase your engagement level in this principle?

Directions: On the next several pages, you will complete your daily log sheets where you will:

- Begin the day by writing an **Affirmation** to **Command Your Day**.

- Complete the daily log by inputting your **Road Map** goals to master this principle that you would like to accomplish for the next five days. At the end of each day, you will assess your progress.

- End each day in a **Spirit of Gratitude** by reflecting on your blessings for the day. Also, you can sum up your day in greater detail by writing in the **Daily Reflection** section of this chapter.

- At the end of the section, you will complete the **Purpose Engagement** form. This will measure your activity level in each of the principles level. Through this process, you will measure your progress and assess your direction into **Living a Life of Purpose.**

- Reflect, revise, and write your experience along this journey on the journal lines provided as well.

Day One: My Daily Affirmation

Today I will,

Day One: Road Map Goals

Goals	Action Taken

Day One: Spirit of Gratitude

Today I am Thankful for:

Daily Reflections:

Day Two: My Daily Affirmation

Today I will,

Day Two: Road Map Goals

Goals	Action Taken

Day Two: Spirit of Gratitude

Today I am Thankful for:

Daily Reflections:

Day Three: My Daily Affirmation

Today I will,

Day Three: Road Map Goals

Goals	Action Taken

Day Three: Spirit of Gratitude

Today I am Thankful for:

Daily Reflections:

Day Four: My Daily Affirmation

Today I will,

Day Four: Road Map Goals

Goals	Action Taken

Day Four: Spirit of Gratitude

Today I am Thankful for:

Daily Reflections:

Day Five: My Daily Affirmation

Today I will,

Day Five: Road Map Goals

Goals	Action Taken

Day Five: Spirit of Gratitude

Today I am Thankful for:

Daily Reflections:

Purpose Engagement Form
Directions:

1. Rate the percentage of time spent in the **Call to Greatness Empowerment** principle
2. Rate your performance and label each **Call to Greatness** principle below, using the following rubric:

1. Poor	2. Fair	3. Good	4. Very Good
		5. Excellent	

Call to Greatness Empowerment Principles	Rate the percentage of your time spent in this principle	Rate your level of performance in this principle on a scale of 0–5
Activate Your Push Power (APP)		

What Fruit of the Spirit do you currently manifest in this principle? Please list below all the attributes that relate. Please explain:

Love	Peace	Kindness	Faithfulness	Self-Control
Joy	Patience	Goodness	Gentleness	None of the above

Second Principle

Developing the Whole Self (DWS)

Second Principle: Developing the Whole Self *(DWS)*

Through this process, you will develop a commitment to **SOAR** into becoming your best self. Within that principle, you will focus on developing your talents, strengths, passions, and establish a career or a calling. Remember that you have seeds of greatness planted within you. You were prepackaged when you came to this earth to complete an assignment. These seeds are your gifts and talents that need to be further developed.

To better understand your **Call to Greatness**, you will need to identify your gifts, strengths, and talents, which will ultimately lead you to **Living a Life of Purpose**. (If you are unsure of your strengths, please visit the Resources page on our website at **www.thepurposefactormovement.com** to complete an assessment).

Walking in your **Call to Greatness** means living a life with intention and direction. Using this guided journal, you will develop a **Road Map**, which will comprise of a plan illustrating your short term, intermediate, and long-term goals. Through this journey, you will develop techniques that will equip you to **SOAR** into **Greatness.** Therefore, with intention and direction you will need to create a **Mission Statement** for yourself. Through this process, you will ask the following questions:
- Who am I?
- What do I enjoy doing?
- What's important to me?
- What are my values and core principles?

You must take the time and write down these answers. In doing so, you will then be able to create a mission statement. For additional help with creating your mission statement, please visit our Resources page at www.thepurposefactormovement.com.

What is Your Mission Statement?

Once your mission statement is complete, it will serve as your guide as you continue on the path of **Living a Life of Purpose**. Whenever a new opportunity or venture comes along, you will need to see if it aligns with your **Mission**. Whenever you are faced with adversity or a setback in any of the other **Living a Life of Purpose** principles, you will need to go back to your **Mission** as well. Your mission will answer any of the *Why* and *What* questions in your life - *Why am I doing this? Why am I on this earth? What is my* **Purpose** or **Call to Greatness**? Finally, your **Mission** will help ignite your **Push Power** and give you the surge to move forward in a positive direction.

Reflections

How would you describe your performance in pursuing your personal goals?

Rate your engagement level of performance within this principle, using the following scale: 0 to 5

- Operating at a **level five** means that you are mastering that principle; you are intentional and engaged in actions that promote your strengths, talents and passion, love and service to others. In addition, you are taking actions that promote continuous advancement, assessments, and reflections within that principle.
- Operating at a **level three** means that you are aware of your strengths, passion or career interest. You are not consistently engaging in actions that promote and develop your goals. On that level, you have a conscious awareness of what to do to increase your performance and you may be making strides toward success in that area.
- Operating at a **level zero** or **one** means that there isn't any type of activity or very little within that principle.

Rate your performance in this Developing the Whole Self principle, below using the following rubric:

Poor	Fair	Good	Very Good	Excellent
0	1	2	4	5

Your Developing the Whole Self level of performance is _____

- Are you satisfied with your performance? Yes *or* No (circle one)

- Do you know or understand who you are? Yes *or* No (circle one)

- What is your calling?

_____
_____
_____
_____
_____
_____
_____
_____
_____
_____
_____
_____
_____
_____

_____

_____

_____

_____

_____

- What are your strengths?

_____

_____

_____

_____

_____

_____

_____

_____

_____

_____

- What are the areas in your life that can be strengthened?

_____

_____

_____

_____

_____
_____
_____
_____
_____
_____
_____
_____
_____
_____
_____
_____
_____
_____
_____
_____
_____
_____
_____
_____
_____
_____
_____
_____

- What Fruit of the Spirit do you currently manifest in this principle? Please list below all the attributes that relate. Please explain:

Love	Peace	Kindness	Faithfulness	Self-Control
Joy	Patience	Goodness	Gentleness	None of the above

Developing your Road Map Plans

1. How can you master this principle over the next week?
2. What are one or two activities that you can engage in within the coming week that will increase your engagement level in this principle?

_____
_____
_____
_____
_____
_____
_____
_____
_____
_____
_____
_____
_____
_____
_____
_____
_____
_____
_____
_____
_____

Directions: On the next several pages, you will complete your daily log sheets where you will:

- Begin the day by writing an **Affirmation** to **Command Your Day**.

- Complete the daily log by inputting your **Road Map** goals to master this principle that you would like to accomplish for the next five days. At the end of each day, you will assess your progress.

- End each day in a **Spirit of Gratitude** by reflecting on your blessings for the day. In addition, you can sum up your day in greater detail by writing in the **Daily Reflection** section of this chapter.

- At the end of the section, you will complete the **Purpose Engagement** form. This will measure your activity level in each of the principles level. Through this process, you will measure your progress and assess your direction into **Living a Life of Purpose.**

- Reflect, revise, and write your experience along this journey on the journal lines provided.

Day One: My Daily Affirmation

Today I will,

Day One: Road Map Goals

Goals	Action Taken

Day One: Spirit of Gratitude

Today I am Thankful for:

Daily Reflections:

Day Two: My Daily Affirmation

Today I will,

Day Two: Road Map Goals

Goals	Action Taken

Day Two: Spirit of Gratitude

Today I am Thankful for:

Daily Reflections:

Day Three: My Daily Affirmation

Today I will,

Day Three: Road Map Goals

Goals	Action Taken

Day Three: Spirit of Gratitude

Today I am Thankful for:

Daily Reflections:

Day Four: My Daily Affirmation

Today I will,

Day Four: Road Map Goals

Goals	Action Taken

Day Four: Spirit of Gratitude

Today I am Thankful for:

Daily Reflections:

Day Five: My Daily Affirmation

Today I will,

Day Five: Road Map Goals

Goals	Action Taken

Day Five: Spirit of Gratitude

Today I am Thankful for:

Daily Reflections:

Purpose Engagement Form

Directions:

1. Rate the percentage of time spent in each **Call to Greatness Empowerment** principle.

2. Rate your performance and label each **Call to Greatness** principle below, using the following rubric:

1. Poor	2. Fair	3. Good	4. Very Good
		5. Excellent	

Determine the balance that exists between the **Call to Greatness** empowerment principles.

Call to Greatness Empowerment Principles	Rate the percentage of your time spent in each principle	Rate your level of performance in each principle on a scale of 0–5
Activate Your Push Power (APP)		
Developing the Whole Self (DWS)		

- What Fruit of the Spirit do you currently manifest in this principle? Please list below all the attributes that relate. Please explain:

Love	Peace	Kindness	Faithfulness	Self-Control
Joy	Patience	Goodness	Gentleness	None of the above

Third Principle

Enhancing Love in all Relationships (ELR)

Third Principle: Enhancing Love in all Relationships (ELR)

Through this process, you will examine the value and impact of all relationships in your life and develop techniques to enhance those positive relationships.

As infants, love is our primary mode of thinking which shifts into a fear state as we begin to experience life's adversities. These adversities are caused by stressors from the past, worries about the future, and angry or unhappy feelings about what happens on a daily basis. Within this fear mode, we tend to simply exist, disconnected with self, and may not be completely engaged.

As we move into **Living a Life of Purpose,** we cannot be defined by our experiences. Past experiences cannot shape our future. We need to move into a mode of complete awareness where we are constantly assessing the decisions we make in life. We need to filter all decisions through the **Fear/Love test,** according to Melissa Ambrosiana in her book *Mastering Your Mean Girl*. In making decisions, you need to ask the following question: **"What would love do?"** Take a minute and ask yourself, **"Am I making this decision out of love or fear?"** The constant practice of this mental shift will reposition you into living in a state of **Love**, where you can make positive decisions for yourself, family, and community.

Some examples of showing love in your relationships are illustrated by Tautges (2011) in his article "37 Ways to Love One Another" in the table below. To learn more about Tautges' "37 Ways to Love One Another," visit our website at **www.thepurposefactormovement.com**

Table 1.0 **Ten Ways to Show Love**

Be devoted to one another	Give preference to one another
Submit to one another	Seek good for one another
Be of the same mind toward one another	Accept one another by showing deference
Speak truth to one another	Forgive one another
Accept one another by withholding judgment	Be kind to one another so as to preserve unity

To master this principle, you will need to reflect on the following:

- **Are you living in a state of Fear or Love?** *Yes or No (circle one)*

- **Give some examples of decisions you have made out of Fear?**

_____

_____

_____

_____

_____

_____

_____

_____

_____

_____

_____

_____

_____

- In what ways can you incorporate the Fear/Love test in your life? Give two examples:

_____

_____

_____

_____

_____

_____

_____

_____

_____

_____

_____

_____

_____

_____

- In what ways are you demonstrating love in your relationships?

Evaluate the relationships that surround you. Are they influencing you in a positive or negative manner?

My circle is my **Village** which consists of a group of individuals whom I trust and who add value to my life. In this **Village**, we are all interdependent. We support each other through our highs and lows and encourage each other to **Push** through the difficult times.

- **Do you have a village? Yes** *or* **No** (*circle one*)
- **Who are your Villagers (the people who make up your circle)?**

_____

_____

_____

_____

_____

_____

_____

_____

_____

_____

_____

_____

_____

_____

_____

_____

_____

Another aspect of relationships is learning how to navigate around negative energies. Sometimes we may be in a rut where we cannot avoid these individuals. They may be in our homes, workplace, or schools. In these instances, we should reflect on the **Call to Greatness Empowerment Model** principles **APP** and **DWS**. Through this process, you need to focus on your **DWS** and using your **APP** power to give you the energy and determination to **Push** past these adversities.

- o **Are you navigating around any negative energy in any of your personal relationships? Yes** *or* **No** (circle one)
- o **How are you demonstrating Love in all your Relationships?**

_____

_____

_____

_____

_____

_____

_____

_____

_____

_____

_____

_____

_____

_____

_____

- What Fruit of the Spirit do you currently manifest in this principle? Please list below all the attributes that relate. Please explain:

Love	Peace	Kindness	Faithfulness	Self-Control
Joy	Patience	Goodness	Gentleness	None of the above

_____
_____
_____
_____
_____
_____
_____
_____
_____

Another aspect of this **Relationship** principle is identifying the **Gate Keepers** in your life. **Gate Keepers** are people who come into your life and usher you into a new season or new phase. **Gate Keepers** can be teachers, mentors, pastors, etc.

o **Who are the Gate Keepers in your life? How have they ushered you to a new level in your life?**

_____
_____
_____
_____
_____
_____
_____
_____
_____
_____

Reflections

Rate your engagement level of performance within this principle, using the following scale: 0 to 5
- Operating at a **level five** means that you are mastering that principle; you are intentional and engaged in actions that promote love in all your relationships. In addition, you are

taking actions that promote continuous advancement, assessments, and reflections within that principle.
- Operating at a **level three** means that you are aware of the need to demonstrate love in all your relationships. Despite that, you are not consistently demonstrating love in all your relationships and may engage occasionally in it. On that level, you have a conscious awareness of what to do to increase your performance and you may be making strides toward success in that area.
- Operating at a **level zero** or **one** means that there isn't any type of activity or very little within that principle.

Rate your performance in this Enhancing Love in Your Relationships principle below, using the following rubric:

Poor	Fair	Good	Very Good	Excellent
0	1	2	4	5

Your Enhancing Love in Your Relationships level of performance is _____

- o Are you satisfied with your performance? **Yes** *or* **No** (circle one)
- o What are the factors that are either contributing to or impacting your drive performance?

_____
_____
_____
_____
_____

Developing your Road Map Plans

1. How can you master this principle over the next week?
2. What are one or two activities that you can engage in within the coming week that will increase your engagement level in this principle?

_____
_____
_____
_____
_____
_____
_____
_____
_____
_____
_____
_____
_____
_____
_____
_____
_____
_____
_____

Directions: On the next several pages, you will complete your daily log sheets where you will:

- Begin the day by writing an **Affirmation** to **Command Your Day**.

- Complete the daily log by inputting your **Road Map** goals to master this principle that you would like to accomplish for the next five days. At the end of each day, you will assess your progress.

- End each day in a **Spirit of Gratitude** by reflecting on your blessings for the day. In addition, you can sum up your day in greater detail by writing in the **Daily Reflection** section of this chapter.

- At the end of the section, you will complete the **Purpose Engagement** form. This will measure your activity level in each of the principles level. Through this process, you will measure your progress and assess your direction into **Living a Life of Purpose.**

- Reflect, revise, and write your experience along this journey on the journal lines provided as well.

Day One: My Daily Affirmation

Today I will,

Day One: Road Map Goals

Goals	Action Taken

Day One: Spirit of Gratitude

Today I am Thankful for:

Daily Reflections:

Day Two: My Daily Affirmation

Today I will,

Day Two: Road Map Goals

Goals	Action Taken

Day Two: Spirit of Gratitude

Today I am Thankful for:

Daily Reflections:

Day Three: My Daily Affirmation

Today I will,

Day Three: Road Map Goals

Goals	Action Taken

Day Three: Spirit of Gratitude

Today I am Thankful for:

Daily Reflections:

Day Four: My Daily Affirmation

Today I will,

Day Four: Road Map Goals

Goals	Action Taken

Day Four: Spirit of Gratitude

Today I am Thankful for:

Daily Reflections:

Day Five: My Daily Affirmation

Today I will,

Day Five: Road Map Goals

Goals	Action Taken

Day Five: Spirit of Gratitude

Today I am Thankful for:

Daily Reflections:

Purpose Engagement Form
Directions:
1. Rate the percentage of time spent in each **Call to Greatness Empowerment** principle.

2. Rate your performance and label each **Call to Greatness** principle below, using the following rubric:

1. Poor	2. Fair	3. Good	4. Very Good
		5. Excellent	

Determine the balance that exists between the **Call to Greatness** empowerment principles.

Call to Greatness Empowerment Principles	Rate the percentage of your time spent in each principle	Rate your level of performance in each principle on a scale of 0–5
Activate Your Push Power (APP)		
Developing the Whole Self (DWS)		
Enhancing Love in all your Relationships (ELR)		

- What Fruit of the Spirit do you currently manifest in this principle? Please list below all the attributes that relate. Please explain:

Love	Peace	Kindness	Faithfulness	Self-Control
Joy	Patience	Goodness	Gentleness	None of the above

Fourth Principle

Being of Service (BS)

Fourth Principle: Being of Service (BS)

Through this process, you will explore the value of making a difference in the lives of others as you progress along the continuum of success. As you make a difference in your life, you will be able to make a difference in the lives of your family, community, and the world at large. Some examples of ways you can **Be of Service** are illustrated in table 2.0. To learn additional ways to be of service visit our website at www.thepurposefactormovement.com

Table 2.0 Ten Ways to Be of Service

Volunteer at a soup kitchen	Put gas in someone's car
Become an organ donor	Put change in a parking meter
Offer the handy man a drink	Send a friend a vase of flowers
Donate used books to the library	Visit someone who is sick
Buy a new toy for a child in the hospital	Talk with your sales clerk

Reflections
Rate your engagement level of performance within this principle, using the following scale: 0 to 5
- Operating at a **level five** means that you are mastering that principle; you are intentional and engaged in actions that promote your service to other people. In addition, you are taking actions that promote continuous advancement, assessments, and reflections within that principle.
- Operating at a **level three** means that you are aware of the need to engage in acts of kindness and service to others.

Despite that, you are not consistently engaging in acts of kindness and service to others. On this level, you have a conscious awareness of what to do to increase your performance and you may be making strides toward success in that area.
- Operating at a **level zero** or **one** means that there isn't any type of activity or very little within that principle.

Rate your performance in this Being of Service principle below, using the following rubric:

Poor	Fair	Good	Very Good	Excellent
0	1	2	4	5

Your Being of Service level of performance is _____

- **Are you satisfied with your performance? Yes** or **No (circle one)**

- **What are the factors that are either contributing to or impacting your drive performance?**

_____

_____

_____

_____

_____

_____

_____
_____
_____
_____
_____
_____
_____
_____
_____

o What fruit of the spirit do you currently manifest in this principle? Please list below all the attributes that relate. Please explain:

Love	Peace	Kindness	Faithfulness	Self-Control
Joy	Patience	Goodness	Gentleness	None of the above

_____
_____
_____
_____
_____
_____

Developing your Road Map Plans
1. How can you master this principle over the next week?
2. What are one or two activities that you can engage in within the coming week that will increase your engagement level in this principle?

Directions: On the next several pages, you will complete your daily log sheets where you will:

- Begin the day by writing an **Affirmation** to **Command Your Day**.

- Complete the daily log by inputting your **Road Map** goals to master this principle that you would like to accomplish for the next five days. At the end of each day, you will assess your progress.

- End each day in a **Spirit of Gratitude** by reflecting on your blessings for the day. In addition, you can sum up your day in greater detail by writing in the **Daily Reflection** section of this chapter.

- At the end of the section, you will complete the **Purpose Engagement** form. This will measure your activity level in each of the principles level. Through this process, you will measure your progress and assess your direction into **Living a Life of Purpose.**

- Reflect, revise, and write your experience along this journey on the journal lines provided as well.

Day One: My Daily Affirmation

Today I will,

Day One: Road Map Goals

Goals	Action Taken

Day One: Spirit of Gratitude

Today I am Thankful for:

Daily Reflections:

Day Two: My Daily Affirmation

Today I will,

Day Two: Road Map Goals

Goals	Action Taken

Day Two: Spirit of Gratitude

Today I am Thankful for:

Daily Reflections:

Day Three: My Daily Affirmation

Today I will,

Day Three: Road Map Goals

Goals	Action Taken

Day Three: Spirit of Gratitude

Today I am Thankful for:

Daily Reflections:

Day Four: My Daily Affirmation

Today I will,

Day Four: Road Map Goals

Goals	Action Taken

Day Four: Spirit of Gratitude

Today I am Thankful for:

Daily Reflections:

Day Five: My Daily Affirmation

Today I will,

Day Five: Road Map Goals

Goals	Action Taken

Day Five: Spirit of Gratitude

Today I am Thankful for:

Daily Reflections:

Purpose Engagement Form

Directions:

1. Rate the percentage of time spent in each **Call to Greatness Empowerment** principle
2. Rate your performance and label each **Call to Greatness** principle below, using the following rubric:

1. Poor	2. Fair	3. Good	4. Very Good
		5. Excellent	

Determine the balance that exists between the **Call to Greatness** empowerment principles.

Call to Greatness Empowerment Principles	Rate the percentage of your time spent in each principle	Rate your level of performance in each principle on a scale of 0–5
Activate Your Push Power (APP)		
Developing the Whole Self (DWS)		
Enhancing Love in all your Relationships (ELR)		
Being of Service (BS)		

- What Fruit of the Spirit do you currently manifest in this principle? Please list below all the attributes that relate. Please explain:

Love	Peace	Kindness	Faithfulness	Self-Control
Joy	Patience	Goodness	Gentleness	None of the above

SECTION THREE
Your Combined Engagement Score

Your Combined Engagement Score

Now that you have learned about each of the principles of the **Call to Greatness Empowerment Model,** we will further explore how you can actively engage in a **Life of Purpose.** In order to create a **Life of Purpose**, you have to be intentionally operating at a performance level of four or higher in at least three principles of the **Call to Greatness Empowerment Model.** You have to be experiencing a level of satisfaction where you are demonstrating two or more **Fruit of the Spirit.**

Your Combined Engagement score describes your overall engagement level in living a **Purpose Filled Life**. The **Combined Engagement** score is made up of the sum of engagement in the four principles in the **Call to Greatness Empowerment Model**. The engagement scale ranges from a high of 5 to a low engagement rate of 0. The total Combine Engagement Score will therefore range from a high of 20 to a low of 0 as well.

Table 3.0 Your Combined Engagement Score

20	16	12	8	4	0
Very High	**High**	**Average**	**Fair**	**Poor**	None at all

- Operating at a **level 20** means that you are living at a very high level of **Purpose** and walking in your **Call to Greatness**. This score demonstrates that you have mastered activities that promote **Developing the Whole Self (DWS)**,

Activating your Push Power (APP), Enhancing Love in all Your Relationships (ELR), and **Being of Service (BS)** to others. In addition, you are taking actions that promote continuous advancement, assessments, and reflections in **Living a Life of Purpose**.

Finally, you feel high levels of love, joy, peace etc. within yourself and further demonstrate these attributes with your interactions with others.

- Operating at a **level 12** means that you are living at an average level of engaging in **Purpose-filled** activities. This score demonstrates that you are engaging at a high level in a couple of the **Call to Greatness** principles, while engaging at a very minimum or low level in other areas. Another engagement classification could be an average engagement level within all four principles of **Developing the Whole Self (DWS), Activating your Push Power (APP), Enhancing Love in all Your Relationships (ELR),** and **Being of Service (BS)** to others. At this level you may not be consistent in taking actions that promote continuous advancement, assessments, and reflections. The manifestation of the **Fruit of the Spirit** may not be consistent and you may experience high and low periods of love, joy, peace etc. within yourself.

- Operating at a **level 8 or below** indicates that there isn't any type or very little engagement within that principle. This phase is called the **Trauma Factor (T- Factor)**, where you may be experiencing some type of hardship in your life such as unemployment, homelessness, etc., or you are unclear of your direction regarding career, passion or strengths. Please visit the Resources page on our website at www.thepurposefactormovement.com to take a self-discovery assessment.

Your **APP** principle has to be operating at a level four or higher for **Purpose** to be achieved. Without your **APP**, your connection to the spirit, you cannot experience **a Life of Purpose**. Once your **APP** is activated the other three principles, **DWS, ELR** and **BS**, work in concert to bring you to a state of living a **Life of Purpose**.

It is important to strive to maintain a **Combined Engagement** score of 12 to live a **Purpose-filled Life**. When you have reached that standard, you will automatically feel the move of the **Spirit** by the manifestation of its fruit flowing in your life and your interactions with others.

How high are you engaging in a **Purpose-filled Life**? To determine this engagement level, you will complete the table below:

- Enter your engagement level from *Reflections* A, B, C, D

- Add all your scores from Reflections A, B, C, D to give you a **Combined Score**

Table 4.0 **Your Engagement Score**

Life Empowerment Principles	Rate your level of engagement in each of the principles on a scale of 0-5
Activate Your Push Power (APP)	
Developing the Whole Self (DWS)	
Enhancing Love in all your Relationships (ELR)	
Being of Service (BS)	
Combined Total	

What is you Combined Engagement Score? _____

- Are you satisfied with your Combined Engagement Score? Yes or No

- In what ways can you better enhance your Combined Engagement Score?

_____
_____
_____
_____
_____
_____
_____

  o What are your thoughts on engaging into a Purpose-filled Life?

_____
_____
_____
_____
_____
_____
_____

The Trauma Factor (TF)

The Trauma Factor (TF)

The **Trauma Factor** occurs when you cannot move along the continuum of **Purpose** due to a state of confusion, hopelessness, and despair in your life. This factor is illustrated by a **Combined Engagement Score of** 8 or below. This score indicates that someone is experiencing a state of hopelessness, despair, and confusion.

During this phase, individuals may become very dry and dead inside, where they lose Joy, Peace of Mind, Patience, Goodness, Mildness and Self-Control. Their faith and connection to the **Spirit** is not constant and they may be simply drifting. These dry places can be the result of several major changes in their lives. Some of us may be in very bad relationships, unemployed, childless, in poverty, faced with racism, making poor decisions, dealing with the death of a loved one, divorce, etc., or we may even be experiencing a major illness. In other instances, we may have all the rewards of this world, i.e. power, wealth, and employment, but may be at a major crossroad in life and feel drained, confused, depressed and have adverse effects in life, which may range from some of the top ten stressors listed in the table below:

Death of a spouse	Marriage
Marital separation	Dismissal from work
Imprisonment	Retirement
Death of a close family member	Change in health of family member
Personal injury or illness	Pregnancy

Table 5.0 **Top Ten Stressors**

According to *Maslow's Hierarchy of Needs*, one may be able to reach the highest level of one's full potential, called **Self-Actualization** when one's basic needs are first met. The length of time one is affected by the **Trauma Factor** depends on persistence of the stressors related to the adverse effects, the impact of support services to help the individual mitigate the situation, and the individual response rate to such intervention. If the stressors are causing severe impact on your daily functions, I would encourage you to seek help immediately to diminish that impact.

How can we sustain Joy, Patience, Kindness, etc., when we are constantly going through several trials which may cause us to go from levels of high and low emotions? An individual's recovery response rate is based on the presence of **Fortitude** in one's life. **Fortitude** means the strength of mind that enables a person to encounter danger or bear pain or adversity with courage.

Devolving your Fortitude relies on several factors:
- Strengthening your connection to the Spirit.
- Finding the correct/relevant resources to help reduce the stressors you are facing.
- Developing a positive mindset about adversity, that this is just a temporary situation and not a lifetime commitment.
- Understanding that adversity comes into our lives to strengthen our journey, we must then develop tools for our toolbox. It's all part of the **Master Plan** in shaping our **Call to Greatness.**

Your **T-score**

The **T-score** illustrates the level of adversity you are facing in the Trauma Factor in relation to a **Purpose filled Life**. If you have a high **T-score,** it will definitely impact you from achieving your purpose. If you have a low **T-score** it means your adversity level may range from a moderate to a low level.

Table 6.0 **T- score**

Engagement Score	20	16	12	8	4	0
T- Score	0	4	8	12	16	20
Trauma Factor	None at all	Low	Moderate	High	Very high	Red Zone

How to calculate your T- score:

To measure your **Trauma Factor**, you will need to determine your **T-score**. To determine that score, you will need to do the following:

1. Identify your *Total Combined* score from Table 3.0 (pg. 154)
2. Subtract that score from 20

Example 1

Total Combined score = 8   **T-score** = 20-8= **12**

Example 2

Total Combined score = 15   **T-score**= 20-15= **5**

What is your T-score? _____

- **In what areas of the Call to Greatness principles was your Engagement Score below three?**

_____
_____
_____
_____

o What are the factors contributing to such?

*Your Three to Six Month
Road Map Journey Begins Here*

Worksheets

Congratulations!

You have completed 20 days of intentionally **Living a Life of Purpose**. Are you satisfied with your weekly engagement levels on the **Purpose Engagement** Forms?

- **Is there a difference in your engagement level from Day 1 of the journey to Day 20? Yes or No and Why?**

_____
_____
_____
_____
_____
_____
_____
_____
_____
_____
_____
_____
_____
_____
_____
_____
_____
_____
_____

Are you more confident in Living a Life of Purpose and fully engaging in the principles? Yes or No and Why

Developing Your Road Map

In this section of this journal, you will develop a **Road Map** to **Live a Life of Purpose for the next three to six months**. In this activity, you will determine the balance that exists between your current **Call to Greatness** empowerment principles.

1. Rate the percentage of time spent in each **Call to Greatness Empowerment** principle.
2. Rate your performance and label each **Call to Greatness** principle below, using the following rubric:

1. Poor	2. Fair	3. Good	4. Very Good
		5. Excellent	

Purpose Engagement Form

Call to Greatness Empowerment Principles	Rate the percentage of your time spent in each principle	Rate your level of performance in each principle on a scale of 0-5
Activate Your Push Power (APP)		
Developing the Whole Self (DWS)		
Enhancing Love in all your Relationships (ELR)		
Being of Service (BS)		
Combine Score		
T- Factor		

- Which principles are you actively engaging in?

_____

_____

- What are the reasons for this engagement?

○ Which principles need improvement?

- What Fruit of the Spirit do you currently manifest in these principles? Please list below all the attributes that relate. Please explain:

Love	Peace	Kindness	Faithfulness	Self-Control
Joy	Patience	Goodness	Gentleness	None of the above

Developing Smart Goals

Now you are ready to challenge yourself towards the next level, living a **Life of Purpose** beyond this book. To begin this process, you will select one or two goals from one or two of the principles of the **Call to Greatness Empowerment Model** that needs improvement. Which goal(s) did you select?

Step 1: Select 2 or 3 areas that need improvement and you would like to focus on during the next 3 to 6 months.

_____

_____

_____

_____

_____

_____

_____

_____

_____

_____

_____

_____

Step 2: Complete Tables 8.1-8.3 with the selected areas of improvement using the **SMART** criteria.

As you develop your goals, verify that they meet the **SMART criteria:**

Table 7.0 **SMART Criteria**

Specific:	What exactly will you accomplish?
Measurable:	How will you know when you have reached your goal?
Attainable:	Why is this goal relevant to your life? Do you have the resources to achieve this goal? If not, how will you get them?
Realistic:	Is achieving this goal realistic with effort and commitment?
Timely:	When will this goal be achieved?

Table 8.1 Developing Goals

Developing SMART GOALS
SMART: Specific, Measurable, Attainable, Realistic, and Timely
Area of Focus #1:_____
What: What do I want to accomplish?
How: How will you accomplish this goal?
Why: Reasons and benefits?
When: Establish a time frame.
Where: Identify a location.

Table 8.2 Developing Goals

Developing SMART GOALS

SMART: Specific, Measurable, Attainable, Realistic, and Timely

Area of Focus #2:_____

What: What do I want to accomplish?

How: How will you accomplish this goal?

Why: Reasons and benefits?

When: Establish a time frame.

Where: Identify a location.

Table 8.3 Developing Goals

Developing SMART GOALS **SMART**: Specific, Measurable, Attainable, Realistic, and Timely
Area of Focus #3: _____
What: What do I want to accomplish?
How: How will you accomplish this goal?
Why: Reasons and benefits?
When: Establish a time frame.
Where: Identify a location.

Your Next Steps

1. Continue **Living your Life on Purpose** by intentionally working to make a difference in your life, that of your family and community.

2. Save this book and review it annually to reposition yourself toward **Living your Life on Purpose**. Use the next few pages to reassess, reflect, and further your goals.

3. Visit our website at **www.thepurposefactormovement.com** to:

    a. Sign up to be a part of the **Purpose Factor Movement** and share your experience of this journey

    b. Sign up for our **Monthly Inspiration**.

    c. Encourage two or three individuals within your **Village** to be part of this **Purpose Factor** movement and purchase this book.

    d. Have your friends sign up for a complimentary consultation at: **www.thepurposefactormovement.com**

Reflections

GLOSSARY OF TERMS

Being of Service (BS)	An empowerment principle where individuals will explore the value of making a difference in the lives of others as they progress along the continuum of success.
Call to Greatness (CG)	A vision for life where you truly understand the reason you were created. This understanding will give you a new lens through which to see your life, your relationships, and the world around you.
Call to Greatness Empowerment Model	Comprises four principles: Activating Your Push Power (APP), Developing the Whole Self (DWS), Enhancing Love in all Your Relationships (ELR), and Being of Service (BS).
Combined Engagement Score	The sum of the engagement level score in the following principles: Activating Your Push Power (APP), Developing the Whole Self (DWS), Enhancing Love in all Your Relationships (ELR) and Being of Service (BS).
Developing the Whole Self (DWS)	A commitment to becoming your best self. Within that principle, you will focus on developing your talents, strengths, passions, and establish a career or a calling.
Enhancing Love in all Relationships (ELR)	An empowerment principle where individuals will examine the value and impact of all relationships in their lives and develop techniques to enhance positive relationships.

Fortitude	The strength of mind that enables a person to encounter danger or bear pain or adversity with courage.
Fruit of the Spirit	Love, Joy, Peace, Patience, Kindness, Goodness, Faithfulness, Gentleness, Self-control (Galatians 5:22-23).
FEAR/Love Test	Filtering all our daily decisions with the question "What would love do?"
Life Changer	One who is intentional in developing a **Road Map** that propels you toward **Purposeful Living**.
Purpose	The reason something or someone was created or why it exists.
Push Power	The drive and activating force for purpose.
Self-Actualization	One may be able to reach the highest level (based on *Maslow's Hierarchy of Needs*).
SOAR	To rise quickly upward to a great height.
Trauma Factor (T-Factor)	A phase where you may be experiencing some type of hardship in your life such as unemployment, homelessness, etc., or you are unclear of your direction regarding career, passion or strengths. Trauma Factor occurs when you cannot move along the continuum of Purpose due to a state of confusion, hopelessness, and despair in your life.
T-score	Illustrates the severity of your adversity in relation to your Purpose.

ABOUT THE AUTHOR

Making a difference in the lives of other people has become Jacqueline's **Life Purpose. Passing the Torch of Greatness** has become a personal mission both in her professional and private life. Developing the whole individual has been the driving force of her career. Through the establishment of LIFE CHANGERS CONSULTING LLC., Jacqueline has been providing Life Empowerment services and Educational consulting for individuals who are ready to develop a **Road Map** to **Soar into a Life of Purpose**. The empowerment services take the form of life coaching, empowerment, and educational workshops and presentations.

Professionally, Jacqueline has worked in the field of higher education for the past 15 years. She has been a strong advocate for students as they navigate through the college environment. With her understanding of student development theory, she has been very methodical in incorporating cognitive, adult development, and learning theories to many of the student development and wellness programming. Through these programs, students are exposed to learning that helps them develop skills to manage the transitions into the college environment, their academic and personal lives.

Jacqueline earned a Bachelor of Arts in Psychology and Criminal Justice, and later, a Masters of Arts in Clinical Psychology, both from American International College. In May 2014, Jacqueline obtained her Doctorate in Higher Educational Leadership from Nova Southeastern University.

For more information about **LIFE CHANGERS CONSULTING LLC PLEASE** visit: **www.thepurposefactormovement.com**

Made in the USA
Middletown, DE
31 March 2017